World Premiere of

CHIGGER FOOT BOYS

A new play by **Patricia Cumper**

T0348059

Co-production – StrongBack Productions and Tara Arts

PLAYWRIGHT'S NOTE

When in 2013 I began researching the events I eventually included in *Chigger Foot Boys*, I knew I wanted to write a play about the participation of African and Caribbean soldiers in World War One so that their lives would not be excluded from the centennial commemorations. What I found made me more determined to bring the complexity and humanity of their stories to the stage, most particularly the British stage. Great events of world history have always reverberated around the Caribbean and World War One was no exception. Men and women who would shape the destiny of the region for the next forty years were galvanized by this world war and the next.

I came back to live in the United Kingdom in 1993 and it wasn't long after that I became aware how pervasive the myths and legacies of empire continued to be in modern Britain. Not only that the people of the former empire had come to live in Britain in their numbers but also that those who benefited most from the largesse of Empire were deeply unwilling – even afraid – to face the actions and events that created their wealth and privilege. To my mind, this fear must be faced. Those events are history and a nation can only be strengthened by acknowledging and making peace with that history.

There is a rule when writing drama that helps a writer avoid exposition: any inclusion of backstory can only be justified by its importance to the action on stage. I like to think that the obverse applies in our day to day lives. We don't understand why we do what we do until we understand what went before. Only when we understand the backstory, can we truly take action in the present day.

Chigger Foot Boys tells the story of unremarkable lives caught up in truly remarkable events. It looks at these events through the eyes not of the powerful, but of the powerless, and points to the moment at which these ordinary people realize that they must create change for themselves. We are in just such a moment now.

Patricia Cumper
January 2017

CAST
(*in order of speaking*):

MEDORA
Suzette Llewellyn

LINTON
Stanley J. Browne

MORTIE
Ike Bennett

NORMAN MANLEY
Jonathan Chambers

ROY MANLEY
John Leader

OFFICER / RECRUITER / FRIEND / SOLDIER / PORTER
Matthew Truesmith

Creative Team	Production Team
Director	Production Manager
Irina Brown	Shaz McGee
Designer	Stage Manager
Louis Price	Davey Williams
Lighting Designer	Assistant Stage Managers
Kevin Treacy	Jonas Eisenbarth & Imogen Adshead
Music / Sound Designer	Carolina Schmidtholstein
Dominique Le Gendre	Lighting Gaffer
Voice-dialect Coach	Signer
Claudette Williams	Jacqui Beckford

For **StrongBack Productions**
Patricia Cumper, Dominique Le Gendre and Pauline Walker

Production Photographer
Richard H. Smith

Filming
Three Blokes Productions

With thanks to Pippa Ailion Casting and Paulette Harris-German

Biographies:

Ike Bennett MORTIE

Ike Bennett is currently a student at The Royal Central School of Speech and Drama where he has featured in *Three Sisters*, *Twelfth Night*, *Blues For Mr Charlie*, *The Country Wife*, *The Orestia*, *Richard III* and *After The Dance* with current production director Irina Brown.

Stanley J. Browne LINTON

Stanley was born in Hackney, East London and trained at Anna Scher's Theatre and Mountview Acting Academy of Theatre Arts.

Theatre credits include Walker Vessels in *The Slave* (Tristan Bates Theatre); Othello in Shakespeare's *Othello* (Lyric Theatre Belfast, three-month tour in Ireland); Aaron the Moor in *Titus Andronicus* (Etcetera Theatre, Edinburgh Fringe Festival – Surgeons hall, Arcola Theatre) and Mr. White in *Reservoir Dogs* (The Rag Factory).

Television credits include Joe in *Twisted Tales* (Channel 4 comedy pilot series); Tracy Burleson in *Killer Clergy* (CBS drama series); Gary in *Silent Witness* and Guy in *The Bill*.

Film credits include Marcus in *Revolution*; Simon in *Love Hate Date*; Jerome Parks in *Meet Pursuit Delange*; The At Guy in *HashTag*; Steve in *The Fall*; Carter Jefferson in *Rough Cut*; The Client in *Roxanne*; King Mouta in *Moremi*; Deandre in *Final Passage*; Gi Jackson in *The Affair*; Leroy in *Free Runner* and Maurice Campbell in *His Father's Son*.

Jonathan Chambers NORMAN MANLEY

Jonathan was born in Kingston, Jamaica and trained at the Arts Educational Schools and The Royal Academy of Music.

Theatre credits include *Jeremy Corbyn*, *The Motorcycle Diaries* (Waterloo East); *Going UP* (Dublin LGBT Theatre Festival); *Make and Model* (Bush Theatre); *Macbeth* (Shakespeare's Globe); *The Lightning Child* (Shakespeare's Globe); *The Atheist* (St James Theatre Studio & The Lion and Unicorn Theatre); *Danny and the Deep Blue Sea* (Southwark Playhouse); *The Ballad of Benny Junior* (Riverside Studios); *The Legend of Bella Rosa* (Tristan Bates Theatre); *Living Under One Roof* (Nottingham Concert Hall) and *Incendiary* (Oval House).

Film credits include *Throw of a Dice* (CVS Films).

John Leader ROY MANLEY

John trained at East 15 Acting School.

Theatre credits include *Peter Pan*, *War Horse* (National Theatre); *Running Wild* (Regent's Park Open Air Theatre); *Romeo and Juliet* (Orange Tree); *Beasty Baby* (Theatre Rites/Polka Theatre); *Alice's Adventures Underground* (Les Enfants Terribles) and *Clown* (Pohang Bada International Festival, South Korea).

Suzette Llewellyn MEDORA

Suzette trained at LAMDA. She made her debut as Viola in *Twelfth Night*.

Theatre credits include *Mr Tiddle Tum Tums & Other Stories* (Riverstage National Theatre); *The Multiple Myrtle Mysteries* (Endless Horizons Ltd); *Hellscreen* (Firehouse Productions); *Urban Afro Saxons* (Talawa Theatre); *Marisol* (Traverse Theatre Edinburgh); *Trinidad Sisters* (Tricycle Theatre); *Whale* (Royal National Theatre); *Belle of Belfast City* (Lyric Theatre Belfast); *Garden Girls* (Bush Theatre); *Golden Girls, A Midsummer Night's Dream, The Comedy of Errors* and *Love's Labour's Lost* (Wolsey Theatre).

Television credits include *The Coroner, Hollyoaks, Scott & Bailey, Catastrophe, Thirteen, Lucky Man, Rockets Island, W10, Holby City, Hope & Glory, Brookside, Surgical Spirit, Doctors, Casualty, Night & Day, Oscar Charlie* and *Black Silk*.

Film credits include *Molly Moon and the Incredible Book of Hypnotism, Bucky, Manderlay, Baby Mother, Playing Away, Sammie & Rosie Get Laid*.

In the 1990s Suzette co-founded the innovative theatre troupe The BiBi Crew. The company is dedicated to producing new writing from an African-Caribbean perspective incorporating, music, dance, comedy and drama. The BiBi Crew toured the UK with 'On A Level' and 'But Stop! We Have Work To Do' and were invited to perform in New York. The BiBi Crew currently perform pop up shows and are working on a stage play to be performed in 2017.

Matthew Truesmith OFFICER / RECRUITER / FRIEND / SOLDIER / PORTER

Matthew started his career as a street performer in Cornwall and then trained on the 3-year acting course at L.A.M.D.A. After some years working as an actor he moved to directing – cutting his teeth as an assistant at the RSC. Over the years he's worked with acclaimed Russian director Karma Ginkas, spent time with William Esper in New York, took classes at The Moscow Arts Theatre and performed alongside the actor Brian Cox in Orson Welles' *Heart of Darkness* for Fiona Banner. He was Head of Acting at GSA and Head of Postgraduate Acting at Mountview Academy of Theatre Arts. More recently he has returned to freelance work and also makes regular appearances on the stand-up comedy circuit in London – where his unique act continues to enthral audiences and fellow comics alike.

Patricia Cumper WRITER

Patricia has been commissioned by Talawa Theatre Company, Carib Theatre Company, The Royal Court and Blue Mountain Theatre.

The Key Game, commissioned and produced by Talawa at the Riverside in 2004, won four star reviews and was included in Time Out's Critic's Choice.

She was artistic director of Talawa Theatre Company from 2006 to 2012 and produced among other plays George C. Wolfe's *The Colored Museum* in the V&A Museum, and Samuel Beckett's *Waiting for Godot*, the first all-Black production in the UK.

She is currently co-artistic director of StrongBack Productions, a company that brings the Caribbean practice of forging one culture from many histories to British theatre.

Patricia was a member of the team of writers on *Westway*, the BBC World Service drama serial, and wrote a five part radio drama series *One Bright Child* that won the CRE radio drama award.

Adaptations to radio include Rita Dove's *Darkest Face of the Earth* and a fifteen part series for Woman's Hour of Andrea Levy's *Small Island*, a ten part series for Woman's Hour of Alice Walker's *The Color Purple* (that won a silver Sony Award); a one hour play based on Zora Neil Hurston's *Their Eyes Were Watching God*, a ten-part adaptation of Toni Morrison's *Beloved* and a two hour adaptation of Marie Ndiaye's *Trois Femmes Puissantes* (that was nominated for the BBC Radio contribution to Diversity award 2016).

Her original play based on the life of Anthony Trollope *Mr.Trollope and the Labours of Hercules* was broadcast in May 2016. She has been commissioned to write a new 45 minute play about five South London women for broadcast in 2017.

Patricia attended The Queen's School in Jamaica and won the Jamaica Scholarship to attend Girton College, Cambridge University where she studied Archaeology and Anthropology. She won college exhibitions for scholarship and earned her Full Blue and was made Ladies Captain of the university's swimming team.

http://www.strongbackproductions.com/team/

www.patriciacumper.com

Irina Brown DIRECTOR

Irina Brown, born and educated in St Petersburg, has lived and worked in Britain for over thirty years, establishing a versatile career as opera and theatre director, teacher, writer and dramaturge. Irina directed at the Royal National Theatre, Royal Opera House, and the London West End. She was Artistic Director of the Tron Theatre, Glasgow and Natural Perspective Theatre Company.

Her theatre credits include Racine's *Britannicus* (Wilton's Music Hall); *The Importance of Being Ernest* (Open Air Theatre, Regent's Park); Tolstoy's *War & Peace at the Circus* (Adaptor/ Director, Giffords Circus); *Jenufa, the play* (Natural Perspective); Edward Albee's *Three Tall Women* (Oxford Playhouse, Guildford, Cambridge); *The Vagina Monologues* (West End and National Tour) and *Further than the Furthest Thing* by Zinnie Harris (RNT; Edinburgh Festival; Tron; Tricycle; British Council Tour of South Africa).

Her opera credits include Andrei Tarkovski's *Boris Godunov* (ROH, Mariinsky, Monte Carlo); Dominique Le Gendre's *Bird of Night* (ROH); Prokofiev's *War & Peace* (Scottish Opera/ RSAMD); and for the Philharmonia Orchestra Shostakovich's *Orango*, Ravel's *L'enfant et les sortileges* and Stravinsky: *TALES* (RFH and the Proms, RAH) as well as *Gamblers* (LPO). Her future work includes Donizetti's *Anna Bolena* (Badisches Staatstheater, Karlsruhe).

http://www.performing-arts.co.uk/clients/directors/irina-brown/

Louis Price DESIGNER

Louis graduated from Central St Martin's School of Art. He is a video designer, and scenographer.

Recent designs include *Mkultra* (UK Tour); *What Shadows* (Birmingham Rep); *The Emperor* (Young Vic); *The Rotters Club* (Birmingham Rep); *Mavra/Renard/Les Noces* (Royal Festival Hall); *The Etienne Sisters* (Theatre Royal Stratford East); *The Funfair* (Home, Manchester); *L'Enfant Et Les Sortileges* (Royal Festival Hall/ Philarmonia); *Bright Phoenix* (Liverpool Everyman); *Orango* (Royal Festival Hall/ Helsinki Festival/Baltic Sea Festival Stockholm); *Unleashed* (Barbican Theatre); *Sluts of Possession* (Edinburgh Festival/Film Fabriek Belgium); *There Is Hope* (UK Tour); *Amphytrion* (Schauspielhaus Graz); *Wings of Desire* (Circa/International Dance Festival Birmingham); *The Resistible Rise of Arturo Ui* (Liverpool Playhouse); and *Beside the Sea* (WOW Festival, Purcell Room, Southbank Centre).

He directed the documentary film *Beyond Biba – A Portrait of Barbara Hulanicki* (SkyArts/ Sundance Channel); and is developing *Exegesis – A Very British Cult* (BBC Wonderland/November Films); and *Black Country* (November Films/ Arts Council). He edited *Best* (Sundance Film Festival) and *In Mid Wickedness* (Tbilisi Film Festival). As Director of Photography *5 Soldiers* Installation (Herbert Gallery, Coventry/Stadtmuseum, Dresden).

http://louisprice.co.uk/

Dominique Le Gendre MUSIC / SOUND DESIGNER

London-based, Paris educated and Trinidad born and bred, composer Dominique Le Gendre has written music extensively for theatre, art installations, dance, film, television and radio drama for BBC Radio 3 and 4. She composed and produced music for all 38 Shakespeare plays recorded for the audio collection *The Complete Arkangel Shakespeare* directed by Clive Brill.

In 2004 she was invited to become an Associate Artist of the Royal Opera House, (ROH2) Covent Garden, who commissioned her full-length opera *Bird Of Night* directed by Irina Brown and premiered in October 2006 at the ROH Linbury Theatre.

Her chamber works and operas have been commissioned and performed by the Royal Opera House Soloists, Philharmonia Orchestra, Manning Camerata, Lontano Orchestra, Tete-a-tete Opera, The Ibis Ensemble, Ensemble du Monde, Picoplatt foundation and Calabash Foundation for the Arts amongst others. She has been Associate Artist to Manning Camerata led by Peter Manning who commissioned her musical setting of Seamus Heaney's *The Burial at Thebes* which was directed by St. Lucian poet and Nobel Lauréat Derek Walcott.

In 2012, with Melanie Abrahams, she co-curated and co-produced the festival "London Is The Place For Me" at The Tricycle Theatre in London celebrating Trinidad and Tobago's 50th Anniversary of Independence. Since 2013 she has been co-artistic director of StrongBack Productions.

http://www.strongbackproductions.com/team/
http://www.dominiquelegendre.com/

Kevin Treacy LIGHTING DESIGNER

Theatre designs include *Romeo and Juliet, Arabian Nights, The Lion, the Witch and the Wardrobe, A Doll's House* – nominated for Best Lighting Design – Wales Theatre Awards (Sherman Theatre, Cardiff); *Unfaithful* (Traverse Theatre, Edinburgh); *The Weir* (Tobacco Factory, Bristol); *Bird* (Royal Exchange Theatre, Manchester); *The Government Inspector* and *Arrah-na-Pogue* (Abbey Theatre, Dublin); *Twelfth Night* (Nottingham Playhouse); *Beside the Sea* (Southbank Centre); *The Seafarer* (Perth Theatre and Lyric Theatre, Belfast); *Macbeth* (Perth Theatre and Tron Theatre, Glasgow); *Blithe Spirit* (Perth Theatre) and *The Nose* (The Performance Corporation) *Irish Times* award for Best Lighting Design.

Opera designs include *The Turn of the Screw* (Buxton Opera and Kolobov Novaya, Moscow); *Faramondo* (Handel Festspiele, Göttingen); *La Bohéme, L'Elisir d'Amore, Carmen, The Magic Flute* (Nevill Holt Opera); *Imeneo, Rodelinda* and *Die Fledermaus* (Royal College of Music); *Macbeth* (Welsh National Opera); *The Flying Dutchman, Salome* and *Agrippina* – winner of Best Design – Dublin Fringe Festival (Northern Ireland Opera); *Stravinsky's Tales* and *Orango* – directed by Irina Brown (Philharmonia Orchestra at the Royal Festival Hall).

Future engagements include *Killology* at The Sherman Theatre, Cardiff and at the Royal Court, London, *Tosca* at Nevill Holt Opera and *Radamisto* for NI Opera. http://www.kevintreacy.com/

Shaz McGee PRODUCTION MANAGER

Shaz McGee is a Freelance Production Manager with extensive experience worldwide.

Her Production Management credits include *Red Velvet* (Tricycle & New York); *Handbagged, Broken Glass, The Price* (All West End); *The Colour of Justice* (West End and National Tour); *The Dwarfs, Kat and the Kings, The Father* (Tricycle Theatre); *Gandini Juggling* (National Tour); *Stones in his Pockets* (Grand Opera House, Belfast); *Momentary Fusion* (International Tour) and *Ra Ra Zoo* (International Tour).

Shaz is delighted to be working with StrongBack Productions for the first time and working with Irina Brown again, having worked with her on *Further than the Furthest Thing* (South African Tour) and *Britannicus* at Wiltons Music Hall.

Davey Williams STAGE MANAGER

Davey is excited to be working on his first show with StrongBack Productions. A Graduate of Goldsmiths College, he began his Theatre career as part of the LX team on Sonia Freidman Productions' Musical *Bend It Like Beckham*. Whilst continuing to focus on creating his own work after performing with his own Theatre company Omnifolk, at the Edinburgh Fringe Festival 2016.

He began his Stage Management Career on the Tricycle's political thriller *The Invisible Hand*, and has since built up a range of experience at reputable venues such as Iford Arts' Garden Opera Festival, to Sadler's Wells and Southwark Playhouse, as well as touring the UK with The Garnett Foundation.

Pauline Walker PRODUCER

Pauline is a freelance theatre producer, creative producer and writer.

Credits include *The Den* (Swan Wharf); *The Altab Ali Story* (Brady Arts Centre); *Show Me Edgware Road* (Rich Mix); *Custody* (Talawa Studio). Pauline is the Administrator and Creative Producer for The Alfred Fagon Award and was the Producer for The London Hub of Sustained Theatre producing a variety of theatre, arts events and symposia. She is currently writing a novel and has a short story published in 2016 anthology *Shortest Day, Longest Night* (Arachne Press).

http://www.strongbackproductions.com/team/
www.paulinedwalker.com

Performances (Mon – Sat, 7.30pm):

22nd – 23rd February (previews)

24th February (Press night)

Mousetrap Theatre Projects Matinees: Thu 2nd March (2.30pm); Thu 9th March (2.30pm)

Matinee: Sat 11th March (3pm)

BSL performance: Fri 3rd March

Q&A's:

2nd March 11.30am

2nd March 2.30pm – post matinee

9th March 2.30pm – post matinee

This production is supported by Arts Council England, Tara Arts, Cockayne Grants for the Arts (The London Community Foundation); The Royal Victoria Hall Foundation, Unity Theatre Trust, Sylvia Waddilove Foundation UK and individual donors.

TARA THEATRE

Artistic Director Jatinder Verma
Executive Producer Jonathan Kennedy
Associate Director Claudia Mayer
Head of Finance Julia Brundell
Development Associate Frances Mayhew
General Manager Alexandra Wyatt
Technical and Operations Manager Tom Kingdon
Digital Communications Co-ordinator Katie Robson
Development Assistant Lauren Harbord
Finance Manager Xiao Hong (Sharon) Zhang
PR Elin Morgan, Mobius

With special thanks to our Makers & Mentors
Elisabeth Smith
The Shinebourne Family
Ausaf Abbas
& all friends and donors who generously support our work.

Tara Arts is a registered charity no 295547
Tara-arts.com

Supported by
**ARTS COUNCIL
ENGLAND**

Tara Theatre re-opened in September 2016 after extensive renovation to create the country's first multicultural theatre building – ancient doors from India, an earth stage floor from Devon and Edwardian-era bricks lining the theatre walls echo the *connected worlds* that are Tara's vision.

CHIGGER FOOT BOYS

Patricia Cumper

CHIGGER FOOT BOYS

OBERON BOOKS
LONDON

WWW.OBERONBOOKS.COM

First published in 2017 by Oberon Books Ltd
521 Caledonian Road, London N7 9RH
Tel: +44 (0) 20 7607 3637 / Fax: +44 (0) 20 7607 3629
e-mail: info@oberonbooks.com
www.oberonbooks.com

A catalogue record for this book is available from the British
Library.

PB ISBN: 9781786821584
E ISBN: 9781786821591

Cover design by Hans de Kretser Associates

Converted by CPI Group (UK) Ltd, Croydon, CR0 4YY.

Characters

MEDORA
Mid-thirties. Attractive and knows it. Strong.

LINTON
Late thirties. Fit. A little vain.

MORTIE
Late teens. Lanky. Honest. A small shadow on his heart.

NORMAN MANLEY
Mid-twenties. Serious. Bright. Thoughtful.

ROY MANLEY
Norman's brother. Late teens. Charming. Restless.
Hungry for life.

*The actors also play a range of other characters
in the flash forwards as necessary.*

1914

A rum bar in Downtown Kingston, Jamaica.

A large room in a wooden building in the colonial style. There is a staircase leading to the upper floor and fretwork above doors and windows to allow air flow, all slightly shabby. Sounds of trams, carts, street vendors passing. Kingston Harbour is nearby.

There is a bar, and seating for customers at a couple of tables. A gramophone is against the upstage wall. The entrance is through swinging double doors from the street. An electric fan circles slowly.

The set must have the ability to become other spaces and places. The sound is heightened, distorted, mixed to create a variety of soundscapes to evoke these other locations.

In Medora's bar.

Early evening.

MORTIE is sitting at one of the tables nursing a glass of sarsaparilla. A hunting rifle lies across the table.

MEDORA, back turned to the entrance, is cleaning behind the bar. LINTON enters, a soldier let out of uniform, hair slick, shoes shiny and hard heeled.

LINTON goes across and puts a record on the gramophone. He sneaks over to behind MEDORA and as the music plays, leans in close and tries to kiss her on the neck. She hesitates for a second then draws away.

MEDORA: Leave me alone.

LINTON: I bathe and put on my very best to take you out dancing and da's the best you can say to me? Shame, woman.

MEDORA: You on leave?

LINTON: A week.

MEDORA: So when you going home to your wife?

LINTON: You don't hear the music? Come dance with me.

MEDORA: You don't see I have customers?

LINTON: *(To MORTIE.)* Oy, youth man, you don't mind if I dance with this woman here?

MORTIE: Me, sah? No, sah.

LINTON: See?

MORTIE: But it seem to me like you need to listen to what the lady saying, sah.

LINTON: You know who you talking to, boy?

MORTIE: You, sah.

LINTON frowns and MORTIE reaches out and casually rests a hand on his rifle.

MEDORA: You and your foolishness. See what you cause?

LINTON: I don't know why I even bother. I have better places than this to spend my money. Give me a rum.

MEDORA: White or red?

LINTON: White. The way I am feelin', a shot of overproof johncrow batty is what I need to settle mi spirit. Boss man, you can shoot that thing?

MEDORA: Leave him. See yu rum here. Sit down and keep your mouth quiet.

LINTON: I ask you a question.

MORTIE: I can shoot the eye out a barble dove at fifty yards, sah.

The song on the gramophone comes to a halt. The crackle and pop of the needle suddenly seems loud in the space as the lights dim a little.

LINTON: A country boy.

MORTIE: Yes, sah. Proud a it, too.

LINTON: Which parish?

MORTIE: Portland.

LINTON: So what you doing in Kingston?

MEDORA: I don't want to tell you again, Linton. If is a fight you come for, go back to Up Park Camp and tell yu sergeant. I'm sure he will be happy to oblige. But in dese four walls, I am the colonel and I givin' an order.

MORTIE: I can look after miself, miss.

MEDORA: Mi don't doubt that, young man. Is this cunnu munnu I worried about. You want another sarsaparilla? On the house.

MORTIE: Sure.

MEDORA goes to get the drink, dragging LINTON with her.

MEDORA: You don't see how business is bad? Why you trying to drive away the one degge degge customer me have?

LINTON: I surprise you open at all.

MEDORA: Times hard. Every mickle make a muckle.

LINTON: I thought you would be with your little old white man this evening.

MEDORA: So that is it. Is jealous you jealous. If the man want to take me out of a now and then and him have the wherewithal to help me buy my own business place –

LINTON: Jealous? You can do what you want to do, sweetheart.

MEDORA: A woman have to look out for herself in this life.

LINTON: Yu have me to make you feel good, baby girl.

MEDORA: Any man can make me feel good for a minute or two. Who going to mind me when me old and tree start grow in mi face? Not you. And yu know it too.

LINTON goes and takes the needle off the record on the gramophone. MEDORA serves MORTIE in silence. The rain starts to fall. MEDORA gets a bucket out from behind the bar and discretely places it where she knows there might be a leak.

The doors swing open and NORMAN and ROY enter, fleeing the rain. Well dressed, energetic.

MEDORA: Good evening, gentlemen. What would you like this evening?

NORMAN: Shelter, first and foremost.

ROY: And the use of your facilities?

MEDORA indicates where to go and ROY scurries off. The rain comes down harder. NORMAN takes out a large handkerchief.

MEDORA: Dry off and then let me know what you drinking.

NORMAN: Looks like we'll be here for a while. The sky was clear when we set out too.

LINTON puts another record on the gramophone. NORMAN sits at a table. Nods at MORTIE.

NORMAN: Fine looking rifle. Winchester?

MORTIE: 1890.

NORMAN: You hunt?

MORTIE: Yes, sah.

NORMAN: I used to go to bird bush and bag a brace of wood pigeon when I was a boy.

9

MORTIE: Wild boar.

LINTON snorts.

NORMAN: In the Blue Mountains?

MORTIE: Yes, sah. Back Rio Grande side.

NORMAN: I hear those boar would trample a man as soon as look at him.

MORTIE: Is better you see dem before dem see you.

LINTON: Wild boar? You?

ROY re-enters.

ROY: So where are our drinks, brother? Two red rum and water, please, miss. What are we talking about?

NORMAN: We have ourselves a hunter in our midst.

ROY: Looking to bag two harbour sharks down here by the dock side? Nobody told you to be careful in Kingston, rifle or no rifle, man? Kingston is not a place for country boys.

MORTIE: I'm nineteen. I can look after miself.

LINTON: Pride always go before a fall, boy.

NORMAN: There's a difference between pride and a justified confidence, I would say. My money would be on –

MORTIE: Mortimer Gray, sah. Everybody call me Mortie.

NORMAN: – on Mortie if we had a boar charging at us.

LINTON: Good 'ting we in a rum bar in Kingston and not in the Portland bush then.

ROY: So you think you could do better?

LINTON: I know, boss man. I know I can do better. Ten years training at Up Park Camp tell me so.

NORMAN: First or Second Jamaica Regiment?

LINTON: First JR, young man. Saw service in Sierra Leone and all down the Caribbean.

NORMAN: And you feel you can outshoot this young man here.

LINTON: Any day of di week and twice on Sunday.

ROY: That sounds like a bet. What you say, gentlemen?

LINTON: Any time you ready. What you want to shoot at?

MEDORA: Linton, a word, please.

LINTON: I talking to the young gentlemen over here, mi love.

MEDORA: I need some help around here. Right now.

LINTON reluctantly goes to behind the bar where MEDORA waits, arms akimbo.

MORTIE: Wild boar can kill me. Chat cyan harm me. When you ready to fire shot, talk to me.

LINTON: Can't say no to a lady in distress, boy. I coming back.

NORMAN: I believe the young man but I value the word of a soldier. Both are men to be respected. Not an easy competition to judge.

ROY: Always the equivocator, Norman.

NORMAN: And you are too anxious to wager the few guineas you have in your pocket.

ROY: I shall be glad when you get on board that ship and sail away, do you know that? I arrange for us to slip away so we don't have to spend your last night in Jamaica listening to Father droning on about his latest law suit and watching Mother dissolving into tears every time she looks at you, her beloved son, and what do you do?

NORMAN: Try to save you from yourself?

ROY: Don't worry about me, brother. I can look after myself.

NORMAN: Yes. Of course you can. You don't need me any more.

ROY: Stop being such a sentimental old girl! We have one last night. What shall we do with it?

NORMAN: I'm afraid I'm not feeling very celebratory, Roy.

ROY: You changing your mind about going?

NORMAN: Of course not. Why would I?

ROY: Of course not.

NORMAN: Oxford. The dreaming spires. An island boy like me? Of course I have to go. I studied hard to win that Rhodes scholarship. I'm not going to give it up now. I shall be on that ship tomorrow morning.

ROY: I'll drink to that.

NORMAN: Any excuse.

ROY: Dutch courage. Why do they call it Dutch? It seems to me liquor gives any man courage, Dutch or otherwise.

NORMAN: It was gin given to men before battle to stiffen their resolve.

ROY: No need for an encyclopaedia with you around. How good it will be when you are gone and I am seen as the clever one.

NORMAN: So is cleverness relative?

ROY: Certainly. For I am your relative and no one thinks me at all clever when you are around. You're made for all that cerebral stuff. I'm a man of the soil, better with dirty hands than an abstract principle.

NORMAN: Sounds to me like you are making excuses in advance for not doing well in your senior Cambridge exams.

ROY: More rum. I need another drink.

The rains intensifies. There is a distant rumble of thunder.

LINTON: Rain coming down. Look like I going to have to stay the night.

MEDORA: With who?

LINTON: You going throw me out into the rain and mud in my best uniform?

MEDORA: What you think your wife would say?

LINTON: You are a cruel woman. So let me ask you something.

MEDORA: What is wrong with you this evening? You more itchy than a tick on cow skin. Who trouble you?

LINTON: Me? Nobody cyan trouble me.

MEDORA: So what you want to ask me?

LINTON: Dis man who help you buy this place, him married, right?

MEDORA: *(Kisses her teeth.)*

LINTON: So the only difference between him and me is the amount of money him have to spend.

MEDORA walks away.

LINTON: Unless is the colour of his skin.

MEDORA: What you come here for this evening? Eeh? You come to provoke me? You have anyt'ing good to say to me? Eeh? Eeh? You have anything but sweet talk to offer me? You don't hear me say go home to your wife?

MORTIE: Everyt'ing all right, Miss?

MEDORA: Fine. Just fine.

NORMAN: I need to talk to you, Roy. There are things that need to be said.

ROY: No. There is nothing. Nothing at all. You will study. Be called to the bar. I will stay here and look after the estate and the parents. When you return it will be my turn to travel the world. Nothing else to be said.

NORMAN: I have put something aside. It isn't much. When I sold the last stand of logwood timber. Should Mother need it. For bills and wages. I wanted you to know. You cannot let Father catch a sniff of it, do you understand? He will spend it on his bloody court cases. Do you understand me, Roy?

ROY: I didn't win any scholarship. I'm not the golden boy. But I see what I see and I know what I know. Nothing much gets past me. I don't know why you think you need to tell me to look after our mother.

NORMAN: I underestimate you.

ROY: Always. You and everybody else. So let's forget it all and enjoy the evening.

NORMAN: You are right.

ROY: I know.

NORMAN: Cheeky.

ROY: Always.

A crack of thunder.

MORTIE: Miss. A word.

MEDORA: Yes, young man.

MORTIE: I was to sail to Port Antonio on the banana boat on the late tide this evening. With this weather, it might not sail 'til morning. You know where I can rest mi head for the night?

LINTON: The Myrtle Bank Hotel just along Harbour Street. Maybe you could go point you rifle at them and make them give you a room.

MORTIE: Myrtle Bank?

MEDORA: Don't listen to him. They don't take people like you and me there.

MORTIE: I could sleep out here, begging your permission. Cold ground don't bother me. In the bush, that is how we sleep.

MEDORA: No need for that. I have a spare room upstairs.

MORTIE: Thank you, miss.

LINTON: You going make a man with a gun sleep in your place whole night? I better stay and make sure.

MEDORA: Make sure of what? Go 'bout you business, man. I can look after miself.

LINTON: You don't know who to trust.

MEDORA: I know exactly who I can trust. *(To MORTIE.)* One and six and the room is yours.

NORMAN: So you are First JR.

LINTON: Ten years service and counting.

NORMAN: So what say you about these rumours of war in Europe?

ROY: Those continentals are always fighting one another. That history is so complicated that it is like a nest of writhing vipers, to my mind. That is not the Motherland's fight. And if England isn't fighting, then we aren't fighting. Isn't that right – ?

LINTON: Linton.

NORMAN: What say you, Linton? Is my brother right? You must have heard something around camp.

LINTON: I am a soldier. Officer says fight, I fight. I do as I'm told.

NORMAN: And if you are told to fight in Europe?

LINTON: An enemy is an enemy, a dead man is a dead man.

ROY: Besides, if England does join the war, with her navy, she will be triumphant. Six weeks. Six month tops.

NORMAN: There have been German ships in Kingston Harbour.

ROY: And Royal Navy ships too, enough to see off any threat.

NORMAN: You're a soldier, Linton. Will there be war?

MEDORA: What you asking him for? All he does is obey orders and then spend his money looking woman, playing dominoes and drinking rum.

LINTON: And you know you can't resist a soldier boy.

MEDORA: Been a long time since you was a boy.

MORTIE: I would fight.

ROY: Pardon?

MORTIE: Sniper. Pick dem off one by one.

LINTON: You think you have what it takes to be a soldier, boy?

MORTIE: Yes.

LINTON: You and who think so?

MORTIE: Police Commissioner. I take him and his sons up into the Blue Mountains to hunt every New Year. He says the British army could do with a man who can shoot like me.

ROY: You know people in high places, young man.

MORTIE: The younger one bruk him foot falling down a ravine. Is me climb down and bring him up, carry him out of the bush to the coast road. When the fever take him, he wouldn't settle with no one else but me so they ask me to come to Kingston with him. Say they will buy me a ticket to go back on the banana boat. I never see Kingston before so I come.

LINTON: So how you wash up in Medora's bar? They never pay you?

MORTIE: Yes.

LINTON: So you can pay for a room in a guest house for the night then. You no need to stay here.

MEDORA: Don't listen to him, Mortie. Dis is my place and you welcome to stay.

NORMAN: What you think of Kingston?

MORTIE: Everything move too fast. People talk too much. Tram rushing up and down. Everybody want something. You can still see where the earthquake mash up the buildings from all dem years ago. Not what mi was imagining.

NORMAN: Kingston will charm the money out you pocket and before you know it, you don't have anything but your two long hands.

LINTON: What happen? Two Kingston gal smile with you and teif you money?

(Laughs.) You is a real country-come-to-town! Is a good thing you get your ticket for the boat ride back for free else them would have that money off you too.

A distant rumble of thunder. Rain patters more heavily for a minute. The lights flicker. LINTON puts a record on the gramophone: 'By the Light of the Silvery Moon.'

ROY: Was she pretty?

MORTIE: Who?

ROY: The girl who pinched the money out of your pocket.

MORTIE blushes.

ROY: Soldier boy just vexed that he can't get his woman to smile with him tonight. Don't pay any attention to him.

MORTIE and ROY share a smile at LINTON's expense.

NORMAN: The weather is restless.

ROY: It's rainy season.

NORMAN: Rainy season rain falls in the afternoon, not after dark.

ROY: Hurricane season come early then.

NORMAN: Just a tropical storm.

MORTIE: Maybe God vex.

LINTON: You going to England.

NORMAN: Yes.

LINTON: To study.

ROY: Law.

LINTON: Family have money. Studying in England.

NORMAN: Scholarship.

MEDORA: That's where I've seen you before. In the Gleaner newspaper. Rhodes Scholar.

ROY: Going to Jesus College, Oxford.

MEDORA: Jesus College.

NORMAN: Yes.

MEDORA: Sounds like you have to say a prayer just to get in.

NORMAN: Not quite.

LINTON: I've been there. On the way to Sierra Leone. Cold. Gray. Funny place. Saw white men sweeping the streets.

NORMAN: All streets need sweeping.

ROY: So we are a soldier, a hunter, a scholar and a lover. Since we not going anywhere in this weather, what you say we buy a quart of my lady's best red rum and play a game of dominoes?

MEDORA: You might as well. Look like the weather setting in. A soldier, a hunter, a scholar and a sweet mouth boy. Wonder who going win tonight?

The record sticks. LINTON goes and moves the needle on.

MEDORA produces a box of dominoes as the men draw seats around one of the tables. As the dominoes fall and LINTON rubs them vigorously on the table, their clacking sound gets louder, harder as the lights change on the stage.

Flash forward.

Recruitment office.

MANLEY stands at attention in front of a British recruiting OFFICER.

OFFICER: Manley.

NORMAN: Yes, sir.

OFFICER: You've presented us with something of a dilemma, Manley.

NORMAN: Not my intention to do so.

OFFICER:

NORMAN: Sir.

OFFICER: A coloured man cannot be an officer in the British Army. Bad for morale, all that.

NORMAN: I understand, Sir.

NORMAN turns to go.

OFFICER: But a Rhodes Scholar studying Law at Oxford. Him we might need. Played sport, Manley? You look useful.

NORMAN: Sir, if I am not to serve –

OFFICER: Not afraid to fight, are we?

NORMAN: No, sir.

NORMAN waits.

OFFICER: Order came down. Make you an honorary white man, Manley. Officer. Let you find your own level. See what the men make of you. That sort of thing. Can't think they'll like it. Oxford trumps common sense is what I say.

NORMAN: Where am I to serve, sir?

OFFICER: Royal Artillery. You report in two weeks. Orders in the post.

NORMAN: Yes, sir.

OFFICER: Dismissed.

NORMAN: Sir.

OFFICER: What is it?

NORMAN: My brother. He intends to serve against my best advice. May I ask –

OFFICER: Not the time for requests.

NORMAN: – if he might serve with me? In the Royal Artillery. If you ask whole villages to serve together in the pals battalions, surely it is possible for my brother and I to serve together?

OFFICER: Already making an argument like a lawyer, eh. Nothing I can do about that, Manley. Ask when you rejoin your regiment. If they accept coloured men. Is that all?

NORMAN: Yes, sir.

NORMAN turns to go. OFFICER goes back to his paperwork.

NORMAN: I am useful, sir. Run the hundred yards in ten seconds. Sir.

NORMAN departs.

A shift of lighting and we are back at the domino game. The men sort the tiles and take up their hands.

ROY: We short one.

LINTON: Medora!

MEDORA: The double six?

ROY: Yes.

MEDORA: House rules, gentlemen. Too much playing dominoes and not enough drinking means the establishment don't make money. Business is business. Ten shillings behind the bar to pay for drinks and the double six is all yours.

NORMAN: You have a head for business, my dear.

LINTON: Eye for money, you mean.

MEDORA: Mr. Garvey say we need to own we own business so we can be free.

LINTON: Nothing free round here.

ROY: Mr. Garvey? You mean the rabble rouser who has the meetings at Edelweiss Park?

MEDORA: You can call him what you want. What he says makes sense to me. You should go and listen to him sometime.

NORMAN: I hear he is a very powerful speaker. Thousands go to listen.

LINTON: The man is an idiot. The world is the way it is and it is not going to change because a few coloured people don't like it.

MEDORA: You want the double six or not?

NORMAN: Roy? Give the lady the money, young man.

ROY: Why me?

NORMAN: You said you were treating me to a night out.

ROY: Like I said, I'll be glad when you get on that damn boat and sail away across Kingston Harbour to the land of cricket and crumpets. You have all that scholarship travel allowance in your pocket. Why don't you pay, old miser?

NORMAN: Somebody in the family has to teach you how to be financially responsible.

ROY grudgingly pays for the double six. MEDORA gives it to him, clears the glasses and exits. ROY poses the double six on the centre of the table. He then takes up his tiles and slams one down in the centre of the table with a sharp crack to begin the game.

Flash forward.

The amplified sound of the domino hitting the table creates the transition.

Men wait in a line to be called by the RECRUITER. The RECRUITER consults a list.

RECRUITER: Mortimer Gray.

MORTIE: Here.

RECRUITER: You again?

MORTIE: Until I get to fight.

MAN 1: We all waitin' here all day. Why you call him furs'?

RECRUITER: You tellin' me my job?

MAN 1: No, boss.

RECRUITER: Just practise signing you name and stop chat. You cyan sign up to join the army drawing an X. Better hope the doctor don't find no sign a yaws, marasme or venereal disease on you, else you going home.

MAN 1: Me, boss? Strong as an ox. I am an upstanding Christian man.

RECRUITER: That's what you tell all the ladies, right? Wait you turn, man.

MAN 2: We been here since first light, boss man. How much longer we have to wait?

MAN 1: Talk up, man. You belly rumbling louder than you voice.

RECRUITER: Gray.

MORTIE: Yes, sah.

RECRUITER: You sure?

MORTIE: Cold cyan kill me, sah.

RECRUITER: It killed couple hundred of our men that sailed to war, sake of a few decent uniforms. Some people might say you done your bit already. No need to put yourself in the way of more suffering.

MORTIE: People dying, sah. By the thousand. Every day you hear of more. Evil is walking the earth and I sitting by di river watching life flow past. Digging yam hill and picking breadfruit and listening to hoot owl whispering about death in the night time. That is not a life for a man that can drop a boar with a shot to the heart. I done see little of the world, sah. And I ready for more. I not afraid to die.

RECRUITER: Boy, how old are you?

MORTIE: Twenty-one, sah.

RECRUITER: You don't even start live, 'bout you ready to die. Report to Up Park Camp day after tomorrow. The next battalion of the West Indies regiment sailing in two weeks. There is no glory in death, boy. Your job is to survive.

MORTIE: Not to fight, sah? Why you do dis job if you don' believe in fighting?

RECRUITER: A year ago, I believed in fighting, I was sure of victory. The Motherland would conquer the Hun, vanquish the enemy. Two years ago, I stood by Victoria Pier and watched our boys sail out of Kingston Harbour with a heart full of pride. But now, when the dead mounting up to numbers I can't even comprehend? Every soldier that come back home is my victory.

MAN 1: You done chat to the mauger boy now, boss? You no see big man waiting to sign up?

MAN 2: You earning a good wage. We want to earn one too.

RECRUITER: You'd be better off cutting cane than going to war, nobody never tell you that?

MAN 1: Yes, boss. Busha tell me that just after him tell me that him haffi cut my wages because of the war effort. I want my chance to fight like a man. Show the King what a West Indian man can do.

MAN 2: I have to go, boss man, before mi wife find out dat mi girlfriend pregnant!

RECRUITER: Bring you pencil and come. Mek a see you sign. If is fight you want to fight, put you rass name on the dotted line.

Medora's bar

The domino game is ending. NORMAN is holding three tiles. The others have one each.

LINTON: What happen, scholarship boy? Cyan match any tiles? Tap twice, and pass, man. Stop pretending like you have something to play. Tup tup, man.

NORMAN looks to ROY who shrugs and shakes his head then reluctantly taps twice on the table.

LINTON: I did know it, man. You holding the last five spot and I am the only man that can release it. See the card you want here now!

LINTON slams down his final tile.

LINTON: Das how you win. Read the game and know which player holding what.

MORTIE: You was matching.

LINTON: What?

MORTIE: You was matching. You only guess that you was holding up his play when him play the double five last time. You never read nuttin'.

LINTON: Who you talking to, boy?

ROY: Best of three. What do you say, gentlemen?

NORMAN: Rub up the tiles, Mortie.

LINTON: Who say I want to play against dis chigga foot boy? You can still smell the wood smoke and cowshit on him.

ROY and MORTIE laugh.

ROY: Unless you're afraid…?

MEDORA: Linton. A minute, please.

LINTON: Woman, don't bother me.

MEDORA:

LINTON: You don't see I playing?

MEDORA:

LINTON: What you want?

MEDORA: I need you to help me out the back for a minute.

MORTIE: I will come help you, miss.

LINTON: Sit your behind down and rub the tiles until I come. I win once and I will win again. The woman can't keep her hands off me.

LINTON goes off with MEDORA.

MORTIE and ROY turn over the tiles. A rumble of thunder and the lights flicker.

Flash forward.

Lighting change. MEDORA fans herself. LINTON enters with his kit bag. As he opens the door shafts of brilliant sunlight stream in.

MEDORA: You said you didn't have to go.

LINTON: Two JR coming home. We have to go to Africa to replace them. Nobody never expect the fighting to last so long. The whole world at war now.

MEDORA: Is not your business. Is a white man war.

LINTON: And I work for a white man's army. The British West India regiment. I cyan choose when I want to be a soldier. If I take the shilling, I have to obey orders. Just doin' my job –

MEDORA: *(Simultaneously.)* Just doin' yu job.

LINTON takes out an envelope and gives it to her.

LINTON: Read this when I gone.

LINTON picks up his bag to go.

MEDORA: Where you think you going?

LINTON: Mi AWOL, Medora. I wanted to come see you. Mi have to get back to the dock before sarge notice I missin'.

MEDORA blocks the door.

MEDORA: I told you, I am the colonel round here. You go when I say so.

She opens the letter. He tries to slip past. She locks the door. Pockets the key. Stands in front of it. He retreats. She reads. She folds the letter and puts it back in the envelope. Puts it down and walks over to LINTON.

LINTON: Medora –

MEDORA slaps him hard.

LINTON: You wasn't supposed to read it –

MEDORA goes after him. He holds her off.

MEDORA: What you take me for? You see me working hard and you think I don't have no heart? How dare you ask me that! How dare you!

LINTON: I never have nowhere else to turn.

MEDORA:

LINTON: I couldn't think of no one better –

MEDORA: You know – you know! – how I feel. You know. And you do me this.

LINTON: Sorry. Come here.

LINTON tries to hold her. She won't let him. Then she gives in.

MEDORA: I don't know if I going to see yu in life again and you don't even have the grace to lie to me, tell me you love me, pretend that you have likkle feelings for me. You ask me to look after you wife and children. I look like a man to you? I look like I made of stone and you can disadvantage me any which way you please? You have no conscience.

LINTON: Give me the letter.

MEDORA: What that goin' to do? You think that you can pretend you never write what you write?

LINTON: Sorry.

LINTON tries to leave. She will not let him.

MEDORA: Always running away. Always full of sweet talk. Well, now you going to have to talk for true. Why you do dis, Linton?

LINTON: Open the door.

MEDORA: Don't test me.

LINTON: What you want, woman? You want me heart outa mi chest? You want me to crawl on the floor and beg you forgive mi?

MEDORA: It would be a start.

LINTON: She and I married young. Before I join the army. Every time I did go home on leave, is like a new pickney born nine months later. Every penny me earn, gone. And when I go home, she look at me like me no have no place there. Like me come to box the bread out of her pickney mouth. She love dem pickney cyan done. But me? So eventually I stop going. And she never send for me.

MEDORA: Is what do all a you man? How come is always the woman fault?

LINTON: I not saying that. But she have her life and I mind mi children. And eventually mi skin ketch fire fi a woman and I understand what love is. But she no have no time for me. Mi no have no money, mi have responsibilities. She have somebody to set her up in a business of her own. But she know me. She know me inside and out and she no pardon any of my foolishness at all. Her tongue hot like scotchbonnet pepper. And I love her the more for it.

MEDORA: Don't lie to me, Linton. Not now.

LINTON: Dem dying over dere, girl. Thousands upon thousands. So many a dem in one day, dem cyan keep track. Dem bury you where dem find you. If di mortar dem don't get you, di gas will. If dat happen to me, what going happen to my family?

MEDORA: So you write a letter and run out the door in the hope that I will feel sorry for you and take your responsibilities on my shoulders?

LINTON: You was supposed to read it when I gone, woman.

MEDORA:

LINTON: You don't feel sorry for me? Not even a little?

MEDORA: You choose to join the army, you choose to go fight a white man's war. That is down to you, not me. I fight my way through life, fix up this place after the earthquake, build up the business, make a life for myself and you want to jump on the back of it like some coomooging likkle mongoose with you macassar oil and you mouth full of chat? Come out of mi place.

LINTON tries to embrace her. She pushes him off and opens the door.

MEDORA: Come out! Go fight fi di same man dem dat won't let you eat at the same table wit' them. Feel sorry for you? You is a joke to me. Wait a minute. Mi have something for you.

MEDORA roots around behind the bar. She finds a pamphlet and shoves it into LINTON's hand.

MEDORA: Missa Garvey's latest pamphlet. You want to give me somet'ing to read? well you read dat!

MEDORA shoves LINTON out and closes the door behind him. She crumples for a moment then pulls herself together.

Light change.

The domino game.

The rain gets heavier. Water begins to drop into the bucket. The sound is loud in the space.

ROY and MORTIE are sorting the tiles for four players.

MORTIE: God seriously vex this evening.

NORMAN: What time do the trams stop running?

LINTON: Week night. They stop running already.

NORMAN: Look like we will have a long and muddy trek to the guesthouse, Roy. We should be getting back.

A huge rumble of thunder and the lights flicker and go out. MEDORA brings over a small 'Home Sweet Home' kerosene lamp and puts in on the table with the domino game. LINTON comes back to sit and takes up its tiles.

LINTON: So you goin' to cut and run, scholar.

ROY: Best of three, soldier boy. We not going anywhere yet.

LINTON: Das how they teach you to talk to your elders, pickney?

NORMAN: Roy.

ROY: I am not a child.

NORMAN: Howdie and t'ankee bruk no square. Good manners cost you nothing.

ROY: You sound like Father.

NORMAN: You are acting the child so I have to.

ROY: Life is for living, brother. Not sitting on the side and considering.

MORTIE: Time to play.

ROY: You and me against the old fellows, Mortie. What you say?

NORMAN: Who you calling old?

ROY: If the mortar board fits –

LINTON: You sure you can stay awake? Is past your bed time.

MORTIE: 'Fraid you 'fraid, man. Play the game.

They begin to play in earnest. The dominoes are slammed down. The sounds of the heavy rain, the drip in the bucket, the wind rattling are all amplified to create the sounds of a distant battle. The stage darkens and a small pool of light gradually emerges.

In the trenches. There are other soldiers around trying to rest. NORMAN walks into the pool of light with a letter in his hand, tries to find sufficient light to read it.

NORMAN: From my brother.

FRIEND: Roy?

NORMAN: Roy.

FRIEND: How is he?

NORMAN: I asked to have him in my regiment but they said no. Preferential treatment. Bad for morale.

FRIEND: Probably better. You've got to keep your wits about you on the front line.

NORMAN: *(Reads.)* He says that he is fine. Among some fine chaps. He thinks he has a guardian angel as men beside him have fallen dead in the mud in the trenches and he has remained unscathed.

FRIEND: There you are then.

NORMAN: Yes.

FRIEND: Yes.

NORMAN: I found it in the pocket of his uniform when they gave me his belongings before they took his body off for burial. Unopened. No stamp. He'd written it a week before. Forgot to post it.

FRIEND:

NORMAN: I can't find words.

FRIEND: So sorry, old man.

NORMAN: Yes.

Silence. NORMAN crumples then straightens, refusing help to do so from his friend. NORMAN is practically shaking from the intensitiy of his effort to collect himself. He puts the letter in his pocket.

FRIEND: It was an honorable death.

NORMAN: Yes.

FRIEND: He was a brave soldier.

NORMAN: Yes.

FRIEND: Don't dwell, old man.

NORMAN: Dwell. Such a good word. Don't live in that terrible place. Find your way out of that state of mind. Don't dwell.

FRIEND: Ask for a day or two. Get out of the trenches. Do you a world of good.

NORMAN: I hear his laughter. Right here. Right now. I hear his laughter. Is that odd? Did I tell you he hung on until I got there? Rode all night. Close to enemy lines. I didn't care. He would have laughed, me riding like the wind. I was always the cautious one.

He was so pale. The colour of that putty they use to seal windows against the rain. Grey. They put a fresh sheet over him when I got there. I thanked them for that, for the effort when so many men lay dying. But the blood leaked through. Like a rose, a water colour, edges fading into the whiteness. I climbed into the bed and held him. Smelt the disinfectant, the rawness of blood and infection. He knew. He tried to smile. He knew I was there. His eyes emptied. Same eyes. My brother's eyes. Just empty.

His feet. Looked terrible. Trench foot. He wouldn't take off his boots when it rained as a boy. Afraid of getting chiggers in his feet from the mud. The skin had come off with the socks, the nurse said. They were the first thing they covered when they wrapped his body. Those poor martyred feet.

FRIEND: Buck up, old man.

NORMAN: I'll just read it one more time. The men will wonder what has happened to me. Just one more time. I said I'd look after him. I was his older brother. I'll look after him. Just one more time. Mustn't dwell.

NORMAN opens the letter again. His hands shake. His eyes won't focus. He keeps trying. He begins to rock. His friend takes the letter from his hands and tucks it in his pocket as he rocks, head bent, in the middle of that pool of light.

Back in the bar.

The drip in the bucket slows. The rain eases.

A domino game has just ended.

MORTIE: *(Yawns.)* Rain easing.

NORMAN: What's the score now?

ROY: Three games to two.

LINTON: I told you. Age and experience will always beat youth and ambition, boys.

ROY: Best of nine.

NORMAN: Time to call it a night, Roy. Mother and Father will be wondering where we are.

LINTON: That's right. You boys need your beauty sleep.

ROY: You wouldn't have won anything if you weren't playing with my brother.

LINTON: A little bantam like you should stop crow when cock-o-walk about.

NORMAN: Enough, you two. It's just a game.

ROY: Just a game?

NORMAN: There are more important things in life.

LINTON: Listen to your big brother and go home to bed. None of you can test me.

NORMAN: None? Really?

MORTIE: Look like cock-o-walk crow too soon.

ROY: That's what he said. Nobody. Nobody can test him.

NORMAN: We're already late back. The old folks will be in bed. We can stay a while longer. You ready, Roy?

LINTON: You leaving with the country boy for my partner? Is handicap you looking to handicap me?

MORTIE: Mek we play every man for himself. Then we will know who is the best.

LINTON: When I come back, let battle commence.

LINTON heads for the toilet.

MEDORA: The law say I soon have to lock up, gentlemen. Another bottle before you go?

NORMAN: You have any brandy?

MEDORA: Is going cost you.

NORMAN: Brandy. Soda to chase it. I think better with a brandy under my belt.

MEDORA: I thought you said it was just a game, young man?

ROY: Soldier made the mistake of suggesting my brother was stupid. Now that was a stupid thing to do right there. Norman doesn't like to lose.

NORMAN: If he is the best, I going to give him a chance to prove it, that's all.

MEDORA: You think I should warn him?

MORTIE: Him is a soldier. Him should be able to see an ambush coming.

ROY: What you say, Mortie? Give each other a little help? *(Touching parts of his face to signify the numbers.)* One, two, three, four, five, six. We can tell each other what we're holding.

NORMAN: We will play honorably, Roy. No cheating.

ROY: Just evening up the odds, brother. Us young ones have to stick together. You and soldier boy are on your own.

The lights flicker back on. The gramophone stutters back into life and plays the last few bars of a song then starts the hiss and pop of a stuck needle. The stage gets brighter and brighter.

Flash forward.

The distant sound of a call to prayer.

Soldiers are standing in line and at attention.

LINTON scurries up to join them. The conversation is whispered while they standing to attention.

SOLDIER 1: One of these days, sarge going ketch you. What was her name this time?

LINTON: Mariam. She smiled at me in the souq. I had to follow her and see what was beneath that yashmek.

SOLDIER 1: And did you?

SOLDIER 2: Shh.

LINTON: Her brothers ran me off. This time.

SOLDIER 2: Oy. Show likkle respect. They reading a commendation to one of the volunteers.

LINTON: Which regiment?

SOLDIER 1: One of your countrymen from the British West Indies regiments.

LINTON: One of the toy soldier.

SOLDIER 1: Sarge coming.

LINTON:

SOLDIER 1:

SOLDIER 2:

LINTON: That man always look vex.

SOLDIER 2: Does Mariam have a sister?

LINTON: I travel solo, man. No passengers.

Voice off orders them to stand down and fall out. They relax.

SOLDIER 1 takes out a packet of cigarettes and LINTON blags one.

LINTON: Wait. Is that him?

SOLDIER 1: The toy soldier?

SOLDIER 2: Could be. Look like it.

LINTON: Oy. Chigger foot boy!

MORTIE enters.

LINTON: You don't hear me calling you, boy?

MORTIE: I know you?

LINTON: Sniper.

MORTIE: Sorry?

LINTON: Is what do you, boy? You no remember? Me give you and your friends a technical defeat in a game of dominoes in Kingston. Is you, man. Grant. No. Gray. Still a long drink of water.

MORTIE: Kingston?

LINTON: So you make it to war. You said you wanted to fight.

MORTIE: Yes.

LINTON: What? You still vex that I beat you?

MORTIE: Jamaica seem like a lifetime ago.

LINTON: You turn inna man. Look at you. Soldier boy now, eeh. So what you get the commendation for?

MORTIE: Killing the enemy. What else. Pick them off one by one from the back of their line as they try sneak into we camp. By the time the front man get to the gate, him never know every man behind him dead as a nit.

LINTON: Now dat deserve a drink. What you say, men?

SOLDIER 1: I prefer to keep my two shilling in my pocket, Linton.

SOLDIER 2: *(To MORTIE.)* Watch yourself with this man, soldier. Him will charm the bird out the trees and lead you into all kinda mischief.

LINTON: Jealousy is a terrible thing in a grown man, you know that?

The SOLDIERS leave.

LINTON: You just arrive? They bringing in soldiers from all over to make up the Egypt Expeditionary Force. One JR was in Sierra Leone when we get the call. Something big on the move.

MORTIE: East Africa.

LINTON: Never been there. An African man always confuse me. They look like me, but they behave like they live in the trees.

MORTIE: What?

LINTON: Oh, yes. That's why they send us to West Africa. Because a West Indian can survive the heat like an African but he thinks like a Englishman.

MORTIE: You really believe that?

LINTON: You don't?

MORTIE: The first time I line up a black man in my sight and pulled the trigger, I was sick for two days. I swear he look at mi as I pull the trigger. Couldn't get his face out of mi head for weeks.

LINTON: Never stop you getting a commendation for picking them off. You is a hero, man.

MORTIE: Was dem or me.

LINTON: You get any news from Jamaica? Every now and then the heat and the sight of a hibiscus or a bougainvillea make me feel like I back home. You ever feel that? Then I hear the call to prayer and I know I far far from home.

MORTIE: When you think the big push going to start then?

LINTON: Why? You ready to fight again a'ready? Enjoy the likkle rest, young boy. Soon time to kill again. You ever go to the souq? Man, you think Linstead Market big, you should see this. Everything on God's earth in there. Including some fine looking women if you use your imagination. I even find out where, if you drop a money in the right hand, we can get a drink of something alcoholic. And is like the officers don't feel easy there, but a Black face like mine fit right in.

MORTIE: You think we goin' go to Europe? Some of the men hear we going to Italy.

LINTON: Why you worrying youself with what is beyond you?

MORTIE: I 'memba you now. Di rum bar down by the Harbour.

LINTON: Maybe we could find a domino game in camp somewhere. One of you toy soldiers mus' have some.

MORTIE: You know that we let you win dat night. You know dat, right?

LINTON: Stop chat shit in me ears. I will play you and anybody you choose with my eyes closed and still beat you hands down.

They exit together.

In Medora's bar

The gramophone is playing 'I'll Sing Thee Songs of Araby'. Lyrical, gentle. All the men are in shirt sleeves. The rum is running low. The rain has stopped and the crickets and frogs of a tropical night are loud.

ROY: Play, man. Stop holding up the game.

LINTON: I'm thinking.

NORMAN: I thought I could hear gears grinding. If you want to give up, all you need to do is pass, man.

LINTON: Funny.

MORTIE: You know you don't have nuttin' to play. It no matter how much you look in you hand, you still don't have nuttin' to play.

LINTON slams down his hand of tiles on the table, creating a clatter that wakes MEDORA who is nodding off by the bar.

MEDORA: You done now?

LINTON: No. Never.

Turns over his tiles and looks at them again.

MEDORA: You losing.

LINTON: Is not over until is over.

ROY: You sweating there, man. You want me to open the door. Get a sea breeze blowing through the place?

MEDORA: Not unless you want a special constable come pay us a visit. I supposed to be closed at this hour.

ROY: Look like you going to have to deal with the heat, soldier boy.

MORTIE: Tup tup and done.

LINTON: Never.

ROY: So you going lock up the game forever?

ROY signals to MORTIE by touching his face and is answered by a slight nod.

ROY: Pass, man. I still have play to play.

LINTON taps twice reluctantly.

ROY: Two five. What you have, Mortie.

MORTIE: Double five. Look at that. Anyt'ing, soldier boy?

LINTON taps.

ROY: Anything, brother?

NORMAN taps.

NORMAN: Just play and stop all the chat.

ROY: Five one.

MORTIE: Look at that. Double one.

ROY: Just tap tap, Linton. No shame in passing.

LINTON: Facety.

MORTIE: And look at this: anybody for a six?

NORMAN: Just finish the game and done.

ROY: I am enjoying this. You enjoying this, Mortie?

MORTIE: Is a good thing I listen when my grandfather teach me how to read the game. Same grandfather dat teach mi how to shoot boar.

ROY and MORTIE slam down their last tiles and win the game.

MEDORA: Ssssh.

MEDORA turns off the light.

MEDORA: Police.

The sound of a police whistle and footsteps going by outside. The footsteps metamorphose into the sound of persistent knocking.

Light fades up. NORMAN, sitting alone, takes a blanket off his knees and goes to answer the door. He returns followed by a college porter.

NORMAN: The room is cold. I meant to light the fire.

PORTER: I'll get the scout to come and do that, sir.

NORMAN: Thank you.

PORTER: The Master of the college asked me to come and have a word.

NORMAN: The Master?

PORTER: See if you needed anything. As you haven't been to hall, sir.

NORMAN: I haven't. You're quite right.

PORTER:

NORMAN: I can't seem to sleep when I should. And then I get completely exhausted and when I wake I am drunk with sleep and if it is crepuscular I don't know whether it is dawn or dusk so I stay where I am until I find out. And by then it is too late, of course. To come to hall.

PORTER: You were seen on the parapet, sir.

NORMAN: Sometimes I can't breathe. I have to be outside.

PORTER: There are letters for you. From Cornwall. I thought I'd bring them for you as they've been in your pigeonhole for a couple of days.

NORMAN: Ah. Thank you.

PORTER: You have family there, sir?

NORMAN: An aunt. My mother's sister. She is a widow.

PORTER: Ah.

NORMAN: I don't want to worry her.

PORTER: This isn't a rustication matter, sir.

NORMAN: I wondered. When they sent you.

PORTER: But your tutor suggested to the master that you should perhaps go and visit if not Cornwall, friends in London, perhaps. For a while. To rest, sir. Resume your studies next term.

NORMAN: No, I have to go back to my regiment. I can't go swanning off to Cornwall when young men are dying. I'm fine. I will be absolutely fine. Thank you for coming. And for the letters. Thank you. I'm fine.

PORTER: If you say so, Mister Manley. I shall tell the Master.

NORMAN shows the PORTER out. When he comes back ROY is waiting on him.

ROY: You are a poor old thing. Wasting away. Climbing onto the roof.

NORMAN: It is all I can do to remember to breathe.

ROY: So are you going to open the letters?

NORMAN: Yes.

ROY: When?

NORMAN: Soon. Soon.

ROY: You always were a sentimental old thing.

NORMAN: You're dead. You have no opinion in the matter.

ROY: So even when I'm dead, you ignore my opinion?

NORMAN: Ignore you? Ignore you? How can I ignore you? You are all I think about.

ROY: Oh, for God's sake, you're not going to go into one of your eternal apologies again, are you? They are very tiresome.

NORMAN: I've been thinking. About the Empire. And why I – why we – had to fight in this stupid war. It is the Motherland. Motherland. It makes you think of something protecting, nurturing, something that will feed us and keep us safe if we are good children.

ROY: The Empire is a huge bloody thing. Tentacles spread all over the world. More an octopus than a mother.

NORMAN: It came to me. So clearly. It is a great turning wheel, with Britain at the hub. Our sugar, Egyptian cotton, Canadian cod, Ethiopian coffee and Indian tea and gold from the Gold Coast, and porcelain from China … don't you see? If the wheel is on balance, everything comes to the centre where Britain takes its share and then is spread along the spoke of the wheel throughout the Empire. The goods go out and the profit flows back.

And those of us that live in the rim of that wheel think we understand the Empire and we believe in the Mother country, that distant benevolent hub. And like children of a distant mother, we do all we can to please her, be the best we can for her. But this war, this war with its endless carnage that spreads like a cancer across the empire, that has unbalanced everything. This time it is not just goods but people arriving at the hub too. And they've seen up close the reality of the great machine they are there to die to defend. Then the wheel spins faster and faster, the war rages on and on, more and more soldiers have to die –

ROY: It's the way of the world, Norman. There is nothing to understand, nothing to explain my death except rotten luck.

NORMAN: No, no. People like us, people who have bought into the illusion that we are better than those around us because the Empire pats us on the head and allows us a little education, we're just grist to the mill. Cannon fodder. And the closer we are drawn to the maw of the machine, the deeper we look into its heart…

ROY: So what did you want Britain to do? Throw up her hands? Fall over backwards and invite the enemy to mount her? You can't undo history just because you don't like it.

NORMAN: I have to understand.

ROY: Stop. These are matters of state. Not for the likes of us. Nothing you will ever do will change the fact that I am dead.

NORMAN: I know. Don't dwell. *(NORMAN tries to smile. Can't)*

It's too late. I can't pretend I didn't see what I saw. I felt the life leave your body as I held you in my arms. I can't let your death be in vain. This mind, these thoughts are the only things I have to hold onto.

So much terror, pain, death. For what? Who benefits? What happens to a little hurricane swept island like Jamaica if the centre of the Empire cannot hold after this great slaughter? Roy? Roy?

ROY fades away as NORMAN sits again and rocks, lost in his own thoughts.

In Medora's bar.

The light snaps on.

MEDORA: Time for you gentlemen to be going.

LINTON: No, no, no. We not finish playin' yet.

MEDORA: Well, I'm done playing with you. Time to go. Look at the country boy. His eyes are closing down.

MORTIE: Mi all right, miss.

ROY: I could do with a little walk. Clear me head before battle recommence.

LINTON: Too much rum and showing off not good for you.

NORMAN: I'll come with you.

ROY: You think I can't manage on my own?

NORMAN: I think I want to win and I need some fresh air to keep me thinking straight.

MEDORA: I going lock the door behind you so knock when you come back.

ROY and NORMAN leave.

MEDORA: You want me show you the room?

MORTIE: Yes, please, miss. We leave Port Antonio before day this morning, so mi body ready to rest.

LINTON: We need four to play dominoes.

MORTIE: Splash some water on mi face and mi ready to play again.

MEDORA and MORTIE leave and go upstairs. LINTON clears the glasses and the empty bottle of rum from the domino table. Lights a cigarette. Picks up MORTIE's rifle and puts it to his shoulder as if to fire it. MEDORA comes back downstairs. He aims it at her then uses it to stop her from getting back behind the bar. She pushes the rifle aside.

MEDORA: You love playin' with fire too much. Put that thing down.

LINTON: You don't know you not suppose to argue with a man with a gun in his hand?

MEDORA: I know that a man not suppose to spend his time handling another man gun.

LINTON: You too quick for me, girl.

MEDORA: Too everything for you.

LINTON puts down the rifle and comes closer.

LINTON: Who trouble you, girl?

MEDORA: You.

LINTON: Is pure love I comin' to you with, you know that.

MEDORA: Life is a joke to you.

LINTON: If I don't laugh I cry. You never hear old people say that?

MEDORA: Him soon dead, Linton.

LINTON: Who?

MEDORA: You know who.

LINTON: Good.

MEDORA: Is him have the title to the building. Everything in here buy in his name. To protect me, him say. But what happen when he dead? Suppose the family come come throw me out?

LINTON: Him dead yet?

MEDORA: No, but –

LINTON: Then what you worrying about, girl?

MEDORA: Bullfrog say what is joke to you is death to me.

LINTON: Come here.

MEDORA: That is your answer to everything.

LINTON: So?

LINTON puts a record on the gramophone and comes back over to MEDORA and bows and puts his hand out. She laughs, curtseys and takes his hand. They dance, slowly. They get closer. Her body softens and he moves in closer.

LINTON: Life, girl. This is real life.

MEDORA: You chat a lot of fart sometimes.

LINTON: You know you love me.

They dance. A knock on the door. It gets louder. Amplified it gets louder.

Flash forward.

LINTON is taking a piss in an army latrine when MORTIE bursts in.

MORTIE: Hide me.

LINTON: Is what do you, man? You don't see a busy?

MORTIE: Dem after me.

LINTON: Who?

MORTIE: Military police.

LINTON: What you do?

MORTIE: You is regular army. You know what punishment dem give out.

LINTON: You not joking.

MORTIE: I box a man down.

LINTON: You?

MORTIE: An officer.

LINTON: You t'ump down an officer? You.

MORTIE: Mi better go.

LINTON: No, no, no. Sorry. Tell me what happen.

MORTIE: Mi never join up for dis. Digging pit toilet, every little half dead Italian soldier feeling him have the right to talk to you like you is his servant –

LINTON: How much time mi haffi tell you, boy? When you in the army, you do what dem tell you to do. Argument done.

MORTIE: You feel good to know that after all your years in the army, all the fighting you do, you end up with a shovel in yu hand digging a long drop for some facety –

LINTON: I don't like it. But I know better dan to argue. What happen?

MORTIE: We out on labouring detail. Digging a line of latrines. The boys talking about how they going catch two scorpion and put dem in the bottom fi bite dem pon dem privates when dis puffed-up little bullfrog of an Italian officer decide him want to order we about.

LINTON: And?

MORTIE: We tell him to talk to our officer. That we don't take orders from him. Him face turn purple. Him start to sweat.

LINTON: You laugh after him?

MORTIE: But no must? Huffing and puffing like a dragon. Vex until his face twist.

LINTON: So you box him down?

MORTIE: No. I was just watching. And eventually him walk away and everybody get back to work. Until me feel a shadow fall cross me and I look up. And he standing over me. Motioning he's ready to piss, I must dig faster. I never pay him no mind. Me keep digging. And me feel somet'ing wet on me hand and me think it was sweat. But di man dem around me real quiet. And me realise is piss the man is pissing.

LINTON: Das when you hit him.

MORTIE: No. I stand back. I thinkin' if I do what I want to do, dem going lock me up. So I look at him. And I smile. And he still pissing, a big old smile on his face. So I look down. Use my hand to measure my boy then hold up the measurement so him can see. Then I look at him little piece of piss pipe and smile. The boys laugh. His soldiers hear the laughing and come over.

LINTON: What I tell you, boy? Do you work and find ways to live life.

MORTIE: Mi never see the fist coming. Him wait till mi wasn't looking. And me stagger. Then him raise him hand to hit me again. So I duck to one side. Dat rile him. Fist start to fly and I duck and dive as best as mi could. One and two jab glance offa me. The boys was shouting say mi mus' stand and fight. Him start fi charge forward and mi never have no choice.

LINTON: You lay him out.

MORTIE: Clean. Is like him was sleeping, him was so far gone.

LINTON: And then all hell break loose.

MORTIE: And me take me foot in me hand and run.

LINTON: To me.

MORTIE: Nobody from my regiment could help me. Mi never know who else.

LINTON: Shit.

MORTIE: Mi in trouble.

LINTON: Serious trouble.

MORTIE: I goin'.

LINTON: Where? Who you think goin' help a Black man running away through the Italian countryside? They going shoot you before they help you.

MORTIE: I lick down an officer, Linton.

LINTON: You haffi turn yuself in.

MORTIE: And end up in jail?

LINTON: Better than digging latrines on labour detail.

MORTIE: Turn myself in.

LINTON: Yes.

MORTIE: What they going do to me?

LINTON: Him start it, and everybody see dat. A week or two in gaol.

MORTIE: No. I goin' run. I know how to live in the bush.

LINTON: You think this is the Rio Grande? You see any bush around here? Dem will say is desertion and den you will be done for.

MORTIE: It no feel right to me.

LINTON: Trust me. I will talk to my officer. Explain.

MORTIE: Mi no know.

LINTON: You stay here. I will go talk to my officer.

MORTIE: Suppose they find me?

LINTON: Climb down in the long drop and hope to God they only come to piss. Wait for me until I come back, boy. This is the army. They have ways of doing things. But at least the rules apply to everyone so you know where you stand. You only make things worse if you run.

In Medora's bar.

The knocking on the entrance door persists. MEDORA goes and opens the door. The Manley Brothers enter.

LINTON: You ready? Country boy! Don't go to sleep. We ready to play.

MEDORA: Hush you mouth, Linton.

MORTIE comes down the stairs, yawning but up for the game.

ROY: Wake up, man. We into the last round now. Time to find out if you are a man or a mouse!

MORTIE: Don't fret about me. I ready.

LINTON: Coffee, darling.

MEDORA: This place look like a restaurant to you? Play the damn game and go home to you yard, man.

They rub the tiles and take up their hands. MORTIE is so sleepy that he begins to nod at the table.

LINTON: You going to have to play a hand with us, darling.

MEDORA: You see me have time to waste playing games?

NORMAN: We should go, Roy. We've overstayed our welcome. If I wasn't sailing tomorrow, I'd arrange to be back here next week to do it all over again. You deserve to a chance to try and win, Linton.

LINTON: Country boy, go lie down. Medora, sit.

MORTIE goes to lie on the floor and MEDORA takes his place at the table. The game begins and is played in deadly silence with LINTON getting more and more agitated until LINTON can't play. LINTON hesitates, frowning.

ROY: Nothing to play, Linton? Medora?

LINTON: Is cheat the two of you cheating. You think I don't know.

MEDORA: Linton –

LINTON: With their big words and easy life.

MEDORA: They are my customers.

ROY: You wasn't too proud to drink our rum, if I remember correctly.

LINTON: Tha's what they were talking about when they go for that walk. How to win.

NORMAN puts a piece down. LINTON takes it up to give it back to him then realises it means he can play and puts it back in the game.

LINTON: I knew somebody was holding onto the sixes.

The game continues. ROY is about to play when NORMAN stops him with a small shake of the head. ROY chooses another tile and plays it.

LINTON: You can't keep a good man down, man. What I tell you?

LINTON slams down his last tile.

LINTON: End of that game.

MEDORA: And gentlemen, end of this evening.

NORMAN: Thank you for a pleasant time, lady and gentlemen. Roy, time to go.

ROY: I will end it as I began, brother.

MEDORA: Upstairs.

ROY leaves to go to the toilet. A little soft light and the beginning of the dawn chorus.

NORMAN: Four o'clock. I didn't realise it was so late.

LINTON: You will have plenty time to sleep on the ship to England, scholarship boy.

NORMAN: No doubt.

MEDORA: Help me get this boy upstairs, Linton.

LINTON: You no hear him say him used to cold ground? You should let him sleep down here.

NORMAN: He is not much more than a child.

LINTON and NORMAN lift MORTIE who is limp in their arms.

Flash forward.

They rest him on one of the tables. The light narrow focuses on him as he lies, still as death. LINTON puts his rifle across his chest. As the focus of the light widens, we see ROY lying dead too. LINTON and NORMAN neaten the young men as if for burial.

They speak almost simultaneously eulogizing ROY and MORTIE.

LINTON: He lied about his age to join the volunteers going to the great war. He had a hand as steady as a rock, an eye as sharp as a hawk and a heart as simple and clean as a river. He wanted to do what was right. He came to me for help and did as I told him. Trusted that he would be treated as honorably as he had lived his life. I promised him to go and tell his mother that he died fighting. Give her his rifle. They told me I must be in the detail that would execute him for his crimes, that he needed to make an example of him. I would not. Sarge nearly fell off his chair in surprise. No one from One JR or his own regiment would. Mutiny was in the air. In the end, Italian soldiers executed him. I heard the shot. The pain was like hot wire through my heart.

NORMAN: I remember the day he arrived in England. I took the train down to Southampton to meet his boat. They'd dodged German ships in the mid Atlantic, he said. Seen airships floating over the channel. He had grown. Settled into his body. Become the responsible man of the family in my absence. When he laughed, you couldn't help laughing with him. The girls always loved him. Even at his age. I was a little jealous. A great knobbly kneed runner with my head buried in the books: I couldn't compete.

LINTON: His mother said she felt it in her waters when he died. Screech owl cried over her house every night for a week. Me arriving with his rifle in my hand at her door was just the confirmation. That's what she said.

NORMAN: There's much to do. Suck the marrow from this education and find a way forward. This war to end all wars has left the ship of Empire listing dangerously. We should not be aboard when she founders.

LINTON: I found that Garvey leaflet in my kit bag. Mash up right at the bottom. Read it. Read it again. And again on the ship home. Old Marcus Mosiah Garvey had a few ting to say. The world changing. Black man have to start think for himself.

NORMAN: Requiescat in pace, frater.

LINTON: Rest in peace, chigger foot boy.

THE END

WWW.OBERONBOOKS.COM

www.ingramcontent.com/pod-product-compliance
Ingram Content Group UK Ltd.
Pitfield, Milton Keynes, MK11 3LW, UK
UKHW020729280225
455688UK00012B/567

9 781786 821584